D0207944

In Your GREENHOUSE
A BEGINNER'S GUIDE

Greta Heinen

Birch Publishing
Langley, B.C.
Canada

Edited by Laurence Grigg
Cover photograph and interior photographs by Henry Heinen
Cover design and illustrations by Jeff DeWeerd

Printed in Hong Kong by Wing King Tong Co. Ltd.

Canadian Cataloguing in Publication Data

Heinen, Greta, 1948-
  In your greenhouse: a beginner's guide

Includes bibliographical references
ISBN 0-9698030-0-1

  1. Greenhouse Gardening I. Title.

SB415.H44 1994   635'.0483   C94-900307-7

FOREWORD

This little book is long overdue in our North American market. Greta and her family's lifelong association with gardening and the greenhouse business unfolds itself in this easy to read text in down-to-earth layman's language.

Purchasing and running one's greenhouse is an intimidating experience for any gardener. However, this book takes the mystery out of greenhouse operation, giving good basic instructions on the best place to site a greenhouse, as well as ideas on the ideal materials from which to build one. Suggestions for inexpensive heating, ventilation and benches all unfold from the years Greta has spent learning how to run her own greenhouse. This makes it possible for the gardener to do the same.

Here are all the points needed to successfully start the beginner out with the best possible productive greenhouse. This publication shares tips with you on how to winter over your favourite fuchsia, how to start your own annual flowers and vegetables from seed, and how to use your greenhouse all summer long to produce the best tomatoes and cucumbers.

Once you have read <u>In Your Greenhouse, A Beginner's Guide</u>, there will be no holding back, since having a greenhouse provides the one missing link that makes gardening a year-round refreshing escape from the troubles of the world. Enjoy.

David Tarrant

ACKNOWLEDGEMENTS

Over the years, I have met many greenhouse gardeners who were looking for a basic beginner's greenhouse book. The book they were seeking needed to answer questions about greenhouses, equipment, plants and growing temperatures. When I discussed this with my dear friend David Tarrant, he encouraged me to write this book.

So, the first person I would like to thank is David for having confidence in my ability, for his constant encouragement, and for writing the introduction.

To Betty Bethiaume at Valley Orchid Partners for taking the time to give a personal tour of her greenhouse and to share her vast knowledge of orchids.

To Jeff DeWeerd for designing the cover and for preparing the artwork and book design. His artistic ability brought this book to life.

To Laurence Grigg, my editor, who spent many hours editing this copy. He was able to take the words and make them flow into book form.

To John DeWeerd, my printing consultant, whose advice and help was much appreciated when the book was at the publishing stage.

To my dear friends, Edna Parker for her assistance in reading the book from a gardener's point of view, and Ron and Alice Glover, for their support and humour in every situation.

To my children, Rick, Veronica, Jason, Christine, Wayne; and to Marie for her little uplifting notes scattered throughout the house.

Last but not least to my husband Henry for always having his camera ready, for shooting rolls of film, and finally for selecting the photographs for this book.

CONTENTS

Clivia, flowers in February

In Loving Memory of

my father   *Cornelis Kruk*
my brother *Jake Kruk*
my friend   *Don Vail*

C H A P T E R
One

CHOOSING A GREENHOUSE

Discovering the enjoyment of outdoor gardening or being successful with specialty plants in the house often leads one to consider a hobby greenhouse. Owning a greenhouse not only provides year round gardening, but it also brings the challenge of growing different varieties of plants.

A greenhouse can be a major investment, and information on greenhouses and equipment for controlling the environment will help a person decide which greenhouse is the most suitable.

STYLES

The traditional peaked or curved roof free-standing greenhouse is still very popular in many gardens. The square or rectangular shape allows for maximum growing space, with benches on both sides and across the back.

Lean-to greenhouses were designed because backyard space was limited. These greenhouses provided for easy access, which was convenient for connecting the necessary power and water. These greenhouses are attached to the garage, garden shed or side of the house, and they utilized the warmth from the heated housewall.

From this concept the design of a patio enclosure was developed. Enclosed patios and balconies made the greenhouse very accessible, yet they could provide a comfortable sitting area on sunny days.

Aluminum and glass free-standing greenhouse

Octagon or circular designs not only have aesthetic appeal, but also a circular layout which makes wheelchair mobility easier for the physically challenged.

STRUCTURES

Greenhouses can be purchased directly from the manufacturer as pre-fabricated kits or as made-to-order structures. Whether the greenhouse is aluminum, wood, metal tubing or PVC, the structural strength of the design is the most important. The greenhouse frame must be able to withstand extreme conditions, such as high winds and accumulated snowfalls. Hanging baskets and sidewall shelving also require the support of a sturdy frame.

Individually controlled venting, glass louvres and screened hinged doors are also an intricate part of the greenhouse design.

Costs may limit a person to a small greenhouse at the start, but there are greenhouse designs that have the possibility of an extension which can be added on at a later date. This also holds true for those who have found that the greenhouse has become too small. In this case, an extension would be a solution.

Many greenhouses are designed in pre-fabricated sections, so if one has to move a greenhouse, it can be easily dismantled.

COVERINGS

Glass has a proven record as a quality greenhouse covering. Not only are plants visible, but they also thrive with a maximum of natural light during the winter months. Some alternatives to single glass are double-walled products like polycarbonate and acrylite which are becoming known in the marketplace. The insulating feature of these panels can reduce heating costs by thirty percen or more. Light transmission is diffused through these coverings, and, in comparison to glass and depending on the product, light transmission can be up to ten percent less.

Greenhouse polyethylene, or plastic, costs less than other greenhouse coverings, but the drawback is that the covering has to be replaced every few years.

Double-walled polycarbonate greenhouse

SITE SELECTION

The most common question is, What is the best location for my greenhouse? First of all, the greenhouse must be situated as close to the house as possible. This not only makes the greenhouse easily accessible, but it also can act as a cost saving measure when bringing in electricity and water lines. Secondly, the experts recommend that the ridge of the greenhouse run east to west. During the winter months, this angle provides maximum light transmission.

This brings us to the next question: How much light is required? For vegetables and flowering plants, 12 hours of light is the minimum. For dormant or resting plants, 6 to 8 hours of winter light is quite sufficient. Growlights can be installed to supplement lighting in the greenhouse.

Ideally, an asset to the greenhouse location is natural shading from a deciduous tree during the spring and summer months. Exposure to high winds will cause a cooling inside the greenhouse, but building a fence or planting a hedge 3-4.5 meters (10-15 ft.) from the greenhouse will provide adequate shelter.

For a few days one should watch the angle of the sun on the selected greenhouse site.

SITE PREPARATION AND FOUNDATION

Part of site preparation involves deciding whether to have container growing, or have soil beds on one or both sides inside the greenhouse. Electricity and water lines should be laid in the ground before the foundation is put in. One item that is easily overlooked are extra outlets for lights, soils cables and fans.

A hobby greenhouse under 9.3m² (100 sq. ft.) can be fastened to a 4" x 4" treated wood beam foundation. For the larger greenhouse a 6" x 6" beam is recommended. Although wood is treated with a preservative, over time poor drainage on the site will deteriorate the wood. In this case, one is advised to prepare a 10 cm (4") deep and 20 cm (8") wide gravelbed for the foundation. Wooden beams can be stacked to increase the height of the greenhouse. The bottom timber provides a solid base, while the second and third beam can be cut out at the door opening. This makes it possible for the door to be dropped into the opening and eliminates a high step as noted in the foundation sketch. There are several advantages in increasing the height of the greenhouse. More room is available for hanging baskets above the bench  and for the option of extra height for raised beds. In addition, this increased base height allows perimeter heating to be fastened to a solid wall.

If one is not growing in soil beds, then pea gravel under the benches is an excellent flooring in the greenhouse. Walkways are 91 cm (36") wide, using 30 cm (12") concrete slabs. A walkway this size will extend under the bench, and one's feet will not rest on the edge of the concrete.

Over the years, I have found that bark mulch or white landscape rocks are not suitable alternatives to gravel. The moist environment in the greenhouse causes algae on the rocks and a breeding area for pests in the bark mulch.

For a more permanent site, concrete slabs or concrete footings may be installed. Concrete footings have a recommended height of 20-30 cm (8"-12"). Bricks or masonry blocks may also be used.

The foundation is according to the exact outside dimensions of the greenhouse; therefore, one must double check the size before getting started.

All foundations must be level and square for easy installation of the greenhouse structure.

BENCHES

Bench sizes are determined by the width of the greenhouse.

For example, a 1.8 m (6 ft.) wide greenhouse layout will have a 61 cm (2 ft.) bench on either side and a 61 cm (2 ft.) walkway. On the other hand, a 2.4 m (8 ft.) wide greenhouse will have 91 cm (3 ft.) benches on either side, a fifty percent increase in growing space. This is important to consider when growing in containers or trying to maximum the growing space in the greenhouse.

Should the bench be a permanent fixture? Benches are in full use most of the year, but if cucumbers and tomatoes are planned for the summer months, the bench area should be removed. Benches designed in sections therefore, are, the most practical for dismantling and storage.

The recommended bench materials are spaced wooden slats or a frame with heavy gauge wire mesh. A comfortable height for benches is 76-81 cm (30"-32"). The openness of these materials will allow air to circulate to plant level, and any excess water will drain away from the plants.

Tiered bench layouts are often used for displays of tropicals and potted plants.

SHELVING AND PLANT SUPPORT

To add extra growing space to the greenhouse, 20-30 cm (8"-12") shelving is fastened to the sidewall glazing bars. Glass, wood or metal are suitable materials for shelving. A double row of shelving can be used, but there must be enough space between the rows for light to reach the plants. Provided there is adequate light, shelving can also be placed under the bench.

Hanging baskets take up a large portion of the growing space; thus the best location is to suspend them from the roof of the greenhouse. The strength of the roof structure must be able to carry this weight. A B.C. Greenhouse is designed so that each glassbar has a slot from which an eyebolt can hang a basket. Single brackets attached to the sidewall can also carry hanging baskets.

CHAPTER
Two

VENTILATION AND COOLING

The main aim of greenhouse gardening is to maintain an even or optimum environment for the plants. Controlling the cooling in the greenhouse is the first step toward attaining that goal.

ROOF AND SIDE VENTING

Ventilation in the greenhouse is not just seasonal, during the spring and summer. Sudden periods of sunshine can cause extreme temperature fluctuations year round. As this happens, heat builds up very quickly and venting is of the utmost importance. Heat build up is caused by the hot air rising and being trapped at the roof peak. The temperature at bench level will also increase. To ensure adequate ventilation in the greenhouse, open venting should be equal to twenty percent of the floor area. Not only are roof and side venting a source of intake air, but louvres and moveable glass panels in a door also serve this purpose.

Roof venting is still considered the best of ventilation systems. A roof vent serves as an escape route, but it also provides a source of cool air intake. Individually controlled roof vents allow the intake of cool air to be a gentle flow to bench level, not a strong force that suddenly lowers the temperature.

Glass louvres or hinged side venting is also very common at the bench level. Plant damage can occur if the plants are placed in the direct path of the cool air intake during the winter months.

Side venting will certainly assist in cooling the greenhouse in warmer seasons. Another location for side venting is below the bench level. The drawback of venting at ground level, however, is the easy access to the greenhouse for pets and other animals. Mesh screening is advisable in this case.

AUTOMATIC VENT OPENERS

It is impossible for someone to be at home all the time to control greenhouse ventilation. To take the guess work out of vent openings, a solar powered automatic vent opener can easily be

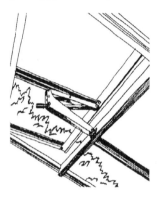 attached to a vent. Automatic vent openers are self-contained units which require no electricity. The unit operates on an expansion fluid that expands and contracts in a cylinder; this in turn activates the vent. On a sunny day, heat will build up around the cylinder mechanism, and the vent will slowly start to open. Similarly, as the air cools around the cylinder the vent will close. These units are available for both roof and side vents. The correct automatic vent opener will depend on the size of the vent and the weight it has to carry.

EXHAUST FANS

Will the greenhouse require an exhaust fan? This depends on the type of venting system that is built into the greenhouse structure, and if there is shading on the greenhouse. If opening the door is the only way one can vent the greenhouse, an exhaust fan system becomes a necessity for proper ventilation. The plant varieties grown in the summer months is a second factor. Depending on the location of the greenhouse, an exhaust fan system may be considered for cucumbers and tomatoes. Speciality greenhouses for orchids, chrysanthemums, or tropicals, require exhaust fans to maintain a controlled environment.

A cooling thermostat and exhaust fan operate electrically on a 110-volt circuit outlet (15 amps). The thermostat is usually set at 30-32°C (80-90°F) in order to activate the exhaust fan. Exhaust fans must have the capacity to exchange the air every few minutes in the greenhouse. Installation of the 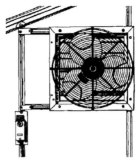 exhausting system must be as high as possible on the back wall.

An 2.4 x 3.7 meter (8' x 12') greenhouse would require a 400 mm (16") low-volume exhaust fan which can draw 950 cubic feet of air per minute. When plants require an increased movement of air, two-speed high volume fans should be installed.

Exhaust fans that are thermostatically controlled can only be used if an equal amount of air intake is available. Without sufficient air intake, the fan will operate at a slower speed, and eventually the motor will burn out. An intake shutter is recommended, but for proper intake it must be two sizes bigger than the exhaust fan. For example, a 400 mm (16") exhaust fan requires a 500 mm (20") intake louvre. Automatic or motorized intake louvres are available in various sizes.

The costs of an automatic exhausting system depends on the size of the fan and the frequency of air exchange.

AIR CIRCULATION

 To equalize the temperature and distribute air evenly within the greenhouse, one should ensure constant air circulation. For the best results, it is recommended that one install a small circulating fan to maintain a continuous movement of air.

As the temperature rises, a lack of air movement creates a stale environment. This in turn encourages fungus growth and other diseases. In spring and summer the fan is located at the bench level, but not in the direct path of the plants.

Air circulation brings down wasted warm air from the peak of the greenhouse to the plant level. During the winter months, the fan should be set at low speed and located near the top ridge of the greenhouse.

Condensation can be greatly reduced if there is constant air circulation.

SHADING

During the spring and summer, direct sunlight can quickly overheat the greenhouse and destroy both plants and seedlings.

Exterior shading is the most effective method of preventing heat build-up. Interior shading will protect the plants from burning, but it still allows the direct sunlight to pass through the covering and to cause heat buildup.

Whitewashing, a term used for painting the exterior covering, is a successful and inexpensive shading technique. A light, translucent coat can be applied in early spring, and the density can be increased as the season progresses. Special greenhouse paints like Kool Ray will lift off with the first frost; then, all that is needed is to wash of the covering. Special greenhouse paints are available for glass, plastic and acrylic coverings.

Shade cloth, or screening material, has been used by commercial growers for many years and is now available for hobby greenhouses. This netted screening acts as a filter for intense sunlight. It can be purchased in different densities, the most common being 65%-70%. Higher density shade cloth is more suitable for orchids or other tropicals.

Bamboo or wood roll-up slat blinds are another shading method. A certain amount of light still penetrates through the blinds, and they can be raised or lowered according to sunlight conditions.

Shade cloth and slat blinds can be attached to the outside of the greenhouse frame, but they must be removed in the fall to provide maximum light conditions during the winter months.

CHAPTER

HEATING AND LIGHTING

An unheated greenhouse serves only as a protective enclosure against the winter climate. The temperature inside the greenhouse will be a few degrees higher than the temperature outside; however, if a cold snap in the weather occurs, the plants will not survive. A little heat provides the *night temperatures* necessary for plants to sustain their growth.

HEATED GREENHOUSE ENVIRONMENTS
Cool or frost free greenhouses maintain a night temperature of 40-45°F (5-7°C). They are suitable for frost sensitive plants and rooted cuttings.

Warm greenhouse require a night temperature of 55°F (13°C). This temperature is suitable for a wider selection of actively growing plants. Growlights are necessary for adequate light conditions in this environment.

Hothouse temperatures are set at 65°F (18°C). Heat and growlights create the natural habitat for tropicals and exotic plants.

HEATING COSTS
Heating costs are the major expense in operating a greenhouse. Warm greenhouses can be twice the cost of a cool greenhouse;

likewise, maintaining hothouse temperatures could triple the cost. Insulating the greenhouse can reduce the heating cost by 30% or more.

INSULATION

Insulation is a greenhouse chore that takes time, but it certainly pays off in savings on the electric bill. To the inside of the greenhouse frame a clear 4 mill plastic liner is fastened, with an airspace between the plastic and the covering. The air space is the insulating factor. Liners can be stapled to a wooden frame, and plastic fasteners are available for aluminum frames. In the colder climates, even if the greenhouse is double glazed, an insulating liner may be added to further reduce heating costs. Vents are also lined with plastic but in such a way that they can still be opened on sunny days. An insulating bubble plastic also serves as a winter liner.

In a cool greenhouse, all dormant plants that are being wintered over can be placed close together in a small heated section of the greenhouse. To section off part of the greenhouse, one needs to install a plastic drop sheet that serves as a partition wall. When plant growth becomes evident and more room is needed, the plastic section can be moved forward to increase the heated section.

HEATING UNITS

Heating requirements depend on the size of the greenhouse, the night temperature required and the expected outside low temperature.

First, one must measure the surface area of the covering, including the doors, and the area of the floor.

Secondly, one must decide the temperature lift that is required. *This is determined from the difference between the lowest expected temperature in the area and the minimum night temperature for the greenhouse.*

There is no need to calculate the different heat losses of various coverings.

Based on this information, a standard equation can be applied for measuring the necessary output of the heater in the greenhouse.

Area in ft.^{2} x temperature lift in $^{\circ}$F x 1.4 = BTU/hour
(3412 BTU = 1 KW)

Area in metres^2 x temperature lift $^{\circ}$C x 7.9 = watts
(1000 watts = 1 KW)

As an example, a 2.4 x 3.6 meter (8' x 12') greenhouse has a floor area of 8.9 meters^2 (96 ft.^{2}), and the covering is approximately 27 meters^2 (290 ft.^{2}) for a total surface area of 36.9 meters^2 (386 ft.^{2}). A 11°C (20°F) lift is required if the lowest temperature expected is -6°C (20°F) and the minimum night temperature is 5°C (40°F). The equation now reads as follows:

386 ft.^{2} x 20°F x 1.4 = 10808 BTU
10808 BTU divided by 3412 = 3.1 KW

35.9 meters^2 x 11 x 7.9 = 3110 watts
3110 divided by 1000 = 3.1 KW

As mentioned above, the heat loss factors in the various coverings are not taken into consideration. If the greenhouse is insulated or double glazed there is approximately a 30% reduction in the required heating output.

An electric heater is the most common source of heat for a small greenhouse. Heaters equipped with a fan assist in the air circulation to distribute a more even temperature. The maximum output of a 110-volt outlet is a 1500-watt heater. Heaters with higher capacities range from 2 KW and up, but require a 220-volt outlet. Most electric heaters are thermostatically controlled with settings of low, medium, and high, or numbers from 1 to 5. Since night temperatures for plants are recorded in degrees, the reading of a maximum-minimum thermometer will help to accurately set the thermostat on the heater. A separate thermostat with accurate temperature readings is available for 1500-watt heaters.

Perimeter heating, with baseboard or tubular heaters, provides an even heat along the sidewalls of the greenhouse. Propane and natural gas heaters use BTU's for heat measurement. These heaters have the output capacity of 12000-20000 BTU's. Kerosene heaters are usually only recommended as a backup heater. These heaters require more attention as well as additional venting.

For safety reasons, it is advisable that an electrician or gas fitter install the heating equipment.

THERMOMETERS

The greenhouse gardener becomes very dependent on a maximum-minimum thermometer. This thermometer records the daytime high temperature and the overnight low temperature. Readings are taken at the bottom of the mercury and are recorded in Celsius and Fahrenheit. This accurate reading advises the gardener of any necessary adjustments to be made to the thermostat controls of the cooling equipment or the heaters. Maximum-minimum thermometers are situated at plant level on the bench, and if plants are growing under the bench, it is advisable to place a thermometer at that level as well.

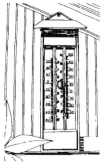

Soil thermometers are used when plants are growing in beds at the ground level. The air temperature and soil temperature will vary. Accurate readings on the thermometer indicate if soil heating cables are necessary in the soil beds. Soil thermometers are also useful for recording soil temperatures in propagating boxes.

SOIL CABLES

A heated propagation area for seedlings and cuttings will save the cost of heating the whole greenhouse. Soil heating cables provide a constant bottom heat for germinating seedlings and root cuttings. The greenhouse is thus maintained at a cooler temperature, which becomes the ideal environment for young seedlings and rooted cuttings.

Automatic soil cables have a preset thermostat of 21° C (71° F). The required length is determined by multipling by three the area of the propagating box or soil bed. These soil cables are available in lengths of three, five, eight and ten meters.

A *soil propagating box* can easily be constructed by building a box 15 cm (6") high around a number of flats. On the solid bottom is put two inches (50 mm) of sand, and the soil cable is laid in looped form. The soil cable is covered with two more inches of sand and the flats 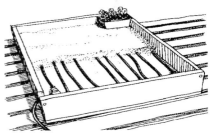 are placed on top. The heat travels through the sand and provides an even heat to the trays or flats. Soil beds or coldframes require a longer cable. These soil cables are not automatic and require a separate thermostat, which has the advantage of various temperature settings. They are available in lengths of 18, 31 and 49 meters.

For propagation, one must be aware of the natural lighting conditions. Since direct sunlight can be harmful, some form of shading is necessary. My mother always taped newspaper to the windows to protect her plants on the window sill. I use the same technique for the small propagating area in my greenhouse during the sunny winter and spring days.

LIGHTING

In a warm greenhouse, the aim is to create the natural

environment for growing plants. Adequate lighting is also a part of this process. Depending on the plants, 12 to 16 hours of light is usually necessary. An automatic timer can be set to add four to six hours of supplementary light to each day.

In a cool greenhouse where plants are dormant or resting, no active plant growth becomes evident until January or February. At this time, depending on the winter light conditions, a few hours of supplementary lighting may be added. Additional light hours give a boost to the cuttings and seedlings. One must keep in mind that the end of May is the earliest that cuttings and seedlings can be planted in the garden.

An efficient growlight fixture is 1.2 meters (4') long and draws 40 watts of electricity. Reflectors on the fixture will direct the light to the plants. The growlight fixture has two tubes, a warm white and a cool white, to give a balanced distribution of light for growth. Each tube has a different function. The cool white tube is high in blue rays. Plants will grow compact with dark leaves, but flowering is not encouraged. Warm white tubes, on the other hand, are high in red rays. Plants will mature early and flowering is encouraged, but plants tend to grow tall. The height of the fixture above the plants is 30 cm (12"), for cuttings 20 cm (8"), and for seedlings 15 cm (6"). The growlight fixture is suspended from the roof of the greenhouse with a linked chain at each end. This makes it easy to raise and lower the height.

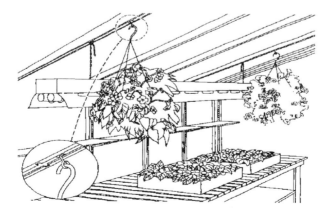

CHAPTER

Four

WATERING AND HUMIDITY

How often plants need to be watered is a question that has no definitive answer. Heat and light are two factors that affect the requirements for watering plants. In a greenhouse environment, the plants can be situated in shade, indirect light or full light; therefore, the watering needs of the plants will differ. Some plants absorb the daily water supply, while others retain moisture for several days.

One can notice when a mature plant needs water because the leaves tend to droop, or the top layer of soil becomes dry. Well rooted, actively growing plants usually need watering each morning and a second evening watering on hot summer days.

The need for watering decreases as plants move into their dormant fall/winter period. At this time watering is only done if the plant requires it. These plants usually need very little water, and, depending on the weather, this could be done once every week or ten days.

It is better to underwater plants than to overwater them. Plants that have been underwatered usually come back to form with the next watering, but an overwatered plant can easily develop root rot and not survive.

WATERING CAN AND SPRAYERS

A plastic one-gallon watering can with a long extension spout and a fine rose-type nozzle is the most suitable for greenhouse

use. The long extension spout makes it easier to reach hanging baskets and the plants across the bench along the sidewalls. A rose nozzle dispenses a gentle spray for seedlings.

To eliminate the difficulty of working with garden hoses in a greenhouse, a coiled watering hose has been developed. This hose can lengthen to 25 feet, and with a long-handled sprayer or wand attached it certainly makes greenhouse watering less time consuming. The sprayer or wands are designed for a shutoff valve in order to control the watering. Nozzles are available for misting and low or high-volume watering .

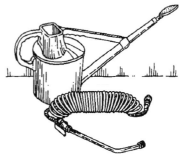

CAPILLARY WATERING

House plants with pot trays for bottom watering are using the capillary self-watering system. *They only draw up the amount of water they require.* In the greenhouse, a sandbed capillary system has produced good results for well-rooted actively growing pot plants. A sandbed can be a portable box with a 7 cm (3") layer of washed sand. Pots are turned so that the bottom of the pot is fitted firmly into the sand. A daily watering of the sand bed keeps the soil moist.

AUTOMATIC WATERING SYSTEMS

Today's watering systems can be automated. The newest addition is small computers which control the time and amount of water to the plants.

Watering kits for hobby greenhouses include tubing, connectors, and drip and mist nozzles. With extra parts, one can also expand an existing system. The connectors are attached to the tap for manual control. With a timer and solenoid valve, the entire system can be automated.

The plant's watering needs always depend on the season. If the system is automated, timers and amounts of water that are dispersed also require seasonal adjustments to prevent overwatering.

Not only is the automatic watering system a time saving device, but it also reassures that, if no one is at home, the plant watering needs will be taken care of.

HUMIDITY

During the winter months, condensation on the greenhouse covering is the first sign that the humidity level is too high. This can occur in a cool greenhouse where plants are dormant and perhaps too moist. Careful watering, ventilation and air circulation will bring down the humidity level.

With increasing temperatures during the spring and summmer, moisture quickly evaporates, causing a drop in humidity that can cause plants to wilt or slow down their growth. One can add moisture to the air by placing cans filled with water in the greenhouse. This is generally enough to bring the humidity up to 60 percent, a comfortable level for mature plants. A cool winter greenhouse has considerably lower humidity levels, but humidity levels rise slightly during the night.

Concrete floors and benches also take the moisture from the air. Several times during hot summer days, one must hose down the floor and benches. This action known as "damping down" not only increases the humidity, but also cools the atmosphere and brings down the temperature.

Tropical plants and orchids require a warm and constantly humid greenhouse environment. A humidifier and humidistat accurately control humidity. The plastic humidifiers sold at local drugstores are quite suitable for greenhouse use.

CHAPTER

SOILS AND FEEDING

SOIL

In any greenhouse environment, success or failure depends on the soil. All soils used in a greenhouse must be sterilized (pasteurized), a process which destroys viruses, bacteria and weed seeds. Sterilization also eliminates any previous plant nutrients.

Local garden centres carry sterilized potting soil and seedling mixes, but one must check carefully the content. Some soils have a peat base and are close to being a soilless mix, so one might try to prepare his or her own soil. The soil can be taken from the garden, or one can purchase a few bags of good topsoil. This is a task I do when the family is gone for the day, because cooking the garden soil can leave an odor. One may use an old roasting pan with a lid to cook the soil in the oven at 177°C (350°F) for about thirty minutes. One must check with a soil or meat thermometer if the centre of the soil has reached 82°C (180°F). Another method is to cook the soil in a microwave. I use a four litre (1 gallon) ice cream bucket covered with Saran wrap and cook it on high for about six minutes. After the soil has been cooked, I spread it out on a flat surface for cooling. Sterilized soil can then be bagged in black garbage bags for future use.

In a larger greenhouse where more soil is required, one should consider investing in a small soil sterilizer. One could also check with greenhouse suppliers for the rental of soil sterilizers.

SOIL MIXES

Peat and perlite are sterile mediums that store water and aerate the soil mix. Soil mix recipes that have proven successful in my greenhouse are the following:

Potting Mix
   3 parts sterilized soil
   2 parts peat
   1 part perlite
   Add 2 tablespoons of 6-8-6 nutirent
      to each 2 gallons (9 litres) of prepared mix.

Seedling Mix
   2 parts sterilized soil
   1 part peat
   1 part perlite
   Add 2 tablespoons of 2-13-0 bone meal to
      each 2 gallons (9 litres) of prepared mix.

Cutting Mix
   2 parts perlite
   1 part peat

It is easier to work with the soil mix if the peat and perlite are dampened. Hot water is used to dampen the peat because it will absorb water quicker than cold water.

PLANT FEEDING

Each number on the boxes of plant nutrients has a different function to encourage plant growth.

Nitrogen	*Phosphate*	*Potash*
(leaf growth)	(root system)	(flower)

Dormant or resting plants have a slow release fertilizer added to the soil mix. The phosphate in the nutrient slowly builds the root system.

As soon as plants show active growth, they require a regular feeding program. Then a question arises: How often do the plants need to be fed? According to the manufacturers' labels on the nutrient box, the application can vary from bi-weekly to monthly feedings. It is recommended that one feed plants more frequently, and this can be done by using diluted doses. If the label recommends one capful bi-weekly, this corresponds to a quarter capful four times during that period. The reason is that, when watering on a daily basis, the nutrients drain out of the container in only a few days. In the early stages of growing cuttings, transplanted seedlings and potted hanging baskets, a root builder of 10-52-17 encourages a strong root system. Once the roots are established and the plants show a steady growth, a balanced feeding of 20-20-20 may be applied. The plants are now starting to grow vigorously, but their root systems still need a boost now and then with a feeding of 10-52-17. Again, it is better to feed more often with diluted doses in order to develop healthy plants.

During an absence for the summer holidays, many gardeners arrange for their plants to be watered but not fed. Granular pellets of 14-14-14 may be placed in pots and containers. The plants will thus have a slow- release balanced feeding when they are watered.

Feeding problems are evident when the plant leaves turn yellow at the edges or have an unusual amount of leaf growth. These conditions are caused by over feeding. Underfeeding produce slower growing plants and a lack of green leaves.

CHAPTER

Six

GREENHOUSE PLANT PROPAGATION

One often visualizes the greenhouse filled with banana trees, orchids and exotic plants growing among bedding plants and geranium cuttings. Many feel we are able to take these plants from their natural environment and create the same climatic conditions in a greenhouse. However, some of these plants are not at all compatible with each other because they each require different temperatures. The *night temperature* in the greenhouse dictates the plant selection, so one must decide whether to maintain a cool, warm or hot greenhouse. Many greenhouse gardeners have made the choice to operate a cool greenhouse simply because of heating costs. Much of this chapter on greenhouse gardening, therefore, deals with this type of environment.

SEED PROPAGATION

The monetary advantages in having one's own greenhouse is very noticeable during the bedding plant season. Depending on the garden size, purchasing bedding plants can be quite costly; yet on the other hand, many plants grow from one seed package.

Seeds can be collected from the best plants in one's garden. These are then stored in the fridge in labeled, sealed jars or zip-lock bags. Seed catalogues are a helpful source of information, especially for the time of maturity. There are special sections in the catalogues for greenhouse seeds of cucumbers, tomatoes and other vegetables or plants that mature in the greenhouse.

Some varieties of slow growing plants are started in January, but the majority of bedding plants seeds are sown in March. The bedding plants started in the greenhouse are not forced but have a "headstart". In this way, they will develop into hardy, well-rooted plants for the garden.

There is always a problem handling very fine seeds, but one solution is to mix the seeds with some dry sand. No matter how hard it is to put a light layer of soil on seeds, some seedlings still come up, pushing the soil into a peak. It is not difficult to make a small handsifter of fine mesh that can disperse a light and uniform top layer of soil.

It is probably more economical to purchase a prepared starter mix for seeds, if one is planting just a few varieties. One can also prepare his or her own seedling mix. In Chapter Five under "Soil Mixes" there is a seedling mix.

Seedlings need a bottom temperature of 21°C (70°F) from a soil cable. The soil cable propagating box will usually carry two or three trays. Plastic seedling inserts are a wonderful invention, and one can place four to eight inserts per flat. Each insert can be sown with a different variety of bedding plant or vegetable seed. Since germination time varies, once the seedlings are ready for transplanting another insert can take its place in the flat. Each insert should be labelled according to variety, colour and sun/shade conditions.

Every gardener has a different opinion on whether to cover the seeds or leave them exposed to light. Personally, I cover all the seeds with black plastic, unless the seed package states that full light conditions are required. I have found that the seeds stay moist during the first few days under the plastic. Since a daily check is made of all the trays, as soon as the seeds germinate, the plastic is removed, and the seedlings are exposed to light. Misting or putting the trays in a water bath are two successful watering techniques.

Seeds only need the bottom heat to germinate, and, as soon as the first set of leaves have developed, they are moved off the bottom heat to a lighter and cooler location. Since the seedlings need as much light as possible, the shelving close to the greenhouse walls is an ideal location. The seedlings always grow toward the light, and the continual turning of seedling trays promotes a more even growth. By thinning out the weaker seedlings, the remaining ones have room to develop stronger roots.

TRANSPLANTING

Transplanting should be undertaken when the second set of leaves, the true leaves, have developed. Seedlings are then gently lifted out by the leaves and transplanted into a sterilized potting mix with 6-8-6 as a nutrient. Depending on the variety of the plant, four to six plants are transplanted into a plastic seedling insert and clearly labelled. For the seedlings to be used in hanging baskets, a second transplant is necessary from the insert into four-inch pots. Transplanting shocks the plant, so they must be stablized by being put into a shaded part of the greenhouse for a day or two.

Because they are in a larger growing space, the watering needs of the plants increases. Continuous plant growth is evidence that the root system is developing. The first feeding that I give to my seedlings contains a very diluted measure of 10-52-17 to further aid the root system.

If the plants become spindly, this could be due to a lack of adequate light. A few hours under the growlights will correct the problem. Many bedding plants can have new branches encouraged by nipping off the growing tip and early buds. "Pinching back" is a practice that is hard to do because the plants are just starting to grow. Plants will become leggy if pinching is not done.

SPRING GREENHOUSE ENVIRONMENT

Spring is the season when there are sudden changes of temperature during the day. Shading the greenhouse is normally done in April, but for the sunny days in March the seedlings need some shade protection. Taping newspaper to the inside of the greenhouse provides adequate shading for the seedlings. When the weather becomes more cloudy, the newspaper may be easily removed.

Circulation and ventilation eliminates stagnant air and is a preventative measure against disease. Individually controlled roof vents are a real asset during the spring season. If one roof vent is automatically controlled, the heat buildup can escape and a sufficient amount of cool air can flow in. When all roof vents open at once, especially in early spring, there will be a sudden temperature drop that can harm seedlings and young plants.

ACCLIMATIZING THE PLANTS

Three weeks before the plants are to be moved outdoors, a period of acclimatizing or "hardening off" needs to take place. This prevents the plants from going into shock and the leaves from turning blue when planted in the garden. Night heat is no longer necessary. Slowly the individual vents are left open during the day, and then one at a time also left open at night. In the second week, all vents, louvres and screens on the doors are left open day and night. One week before the plants are planted in the garden, all the plants should be moved outdoors. If there are still a few cold nights, an open-ended clear plastic canopy can protect the plants. Coldframes are ideal to store plants during this hardening off period. There is no heat, and the lid or vents can be left open.

In the warmer climates, the third week of May is the time to plant the bedding plants. If the spring has been cool and wet, one should wait an extra week. Planting is done in June in the cooler climates. Again, the time in June is dependent on the weather conditions. It is always better to plant bedding plants later because in unsettled weather the plants go into shock and are set back by fluctuating temperatures.

CHAPTER

Seven

GERANIUMS, FUCHSIAS, BEGONIAS AND HANGING BASKETS

Many greenhouse gardeners have successfully grown plants like geraniums, fuchsias and begonias in a cool greenhouse. The good results from the first year quickly expand into a wide selection of cuttings the following year.

CUTTINGS

Pelargoniums, better known as geraniums, and fuchsias are softwood cuttings. August is the month when the plants are fully matured. This is the best time to take cuttings. The high summer temperatures encourage the cuttings to take root quickly. Cuttings can also be taken in the spring and fall, but they require bottom heat in order to root.

A cutting is a new seasonal growth of four to six inches. The size of the parent plant determines the cutting length. A straight cut, with a sharp razor blade or knife, is made just below a node or leaf joint. Then, all the leaves are removed, except the top growth, and dipped into a softwood rooting hormone. The rooting hormone seals off the base of the cutting and also stimulates the roots.

As one prepares the flats or trays, lining the them with newspaper helps to retain moisture. Cuttings can then be placed in a sterile medium of soil, peat, perlite, sand or vermiculite. A perlite and peat cutting mix is listed in Chapter Five under "Soil Mixes". Individual peat pellets are an alternative to preparing a cutting mix. I have had success using these pellets as a cutting medium.

Roots develop at the base of the cutting, so the cutting must be pressed firmly until one can feel the bottom of the flat. By so doing, I have experienced fewer problems with root rot. The plants must be kept moist but not overwatered. All cuttings prefer shade and not direct sun. If the cuttings look healthy, they are developing roots, and in a few weeks they will be ready for transplanting.

PARENT PLANTS

The cuttings are taken from a healthy parent plant that has bloomed continually all season. This parent plant is brought into the greenhouse and allowed to winter over; it will produce more cuttings for spring. The parent plant should be lifted and the stems cut back to within six inches from the base. I usually remove the remaining leaves as well because they will discolour and eventually fall off. Then, the well-developed root system is cut back to six inches from the base. This extensive root system is no longer

required to sustain the plant growth. The parent plant is potted in a sterilized potting soil in the smallest pot that can hold the remaining roots. Parent plants need the same wintering over care as other cuttings.

POTTING THE CUTTING

Well-rooted cuttings are potted into 4" pots in sterilized potting soil with a slow release fertilizer. During the fall and winter, they are in a dormant stage when roots continue to develop and when there is very little growth in the leaves. In late January and February, the daylight hours become longer and the greenhouse daytime temperature becomes warmer. Watering is slowly increased because there are noticeable signs of more active leaf growth. The cuttings are in more soil, so to continue to expand their root system, diluted feeding of 10-52-17 needs to be added to the water.

PINCHING BACK

It is important to "pinch back" the growing tip of the plant to force new shoots and make the cutting into a shaped plant.

Fuchsias are pinched back in the early stage of growth, usually after the second or third set of true leaves. Once it is decided that the fuchsia has enough new branches, the plant can continue to grow undisturbed. It takes up to six or eight weeks after the last pinching back for the fuchsia to bloom.

Geraniums are also pinched back because they tend to become spindly, especially if there is not much sunlight. All the pinching back should be done at the same time so that all the plants will bloom at the same time. Turning the plants weekly also gives the plant an even leaf growth.

TRANSPLANTING TO PERMANENT CONTAINERS

More time is spent by the gardener in the greenhouse and the garden once the plants are in their permanent containers. One must water cautiously as the plants do not absorb as much water in spring as they do on hot sunny days. Again, because the plants are potted into larger containers, a few diluted feedings of 10-52-17 is required for the roots. As the weather becomes sunnier and warmer, watering increases, and diluted but balanced feedings of 20-20-20 bring the plants to maturity.

Marguerite daisies and fibrous begonias are two additional plants that do well as cuttings.

TUBEROUS BEGONIAS

Geranium and fuchsia growers often choose begonias as companion plants in the greenhouse.These plants are noted for their array of colours and long lasting blooms.

Begonia tubers can be purchased and potted up in the greenhouse as early as February in the Pacific coastal region and March in cooler climates. Tubers that have wintered over from last year may show signs of growth as early as January and can be potted up. These plants grow slowly and need time for root development and leaf growth.

When selecting a tuber, one should note that the centre is hollowed out and has some green or pink growth. Moisten the tuber in warm water before planting. An easy method to set this tuber is to use a small pot three quarters filled with moist peat. Then the tuber is twisted firmly in place with the growth tip up but leaving the top exposed. The tuber must be kept moist and the pot placed on a soil cable for bottom heat. Once the roots are developed, and there is a couple of inches of leaf growth, they are gently lifted out and potted into their final containers or baskets.

SOIL MIX

The soil mix begonias prefer is a light mix that drains quickly. This mix consists of peat, sterilized soil, perlite and a little bone meal. To test if the soil mix drains well, one can put some of the mix in a pot and pour water on it. Too much peat causes the water to sit on the top. In this case, adding more soil and perlite makes the soil lighter. Another option is purchasing a prepared soilless mix.

UPRIGHT BEGONIAS

Upright begonias are known for their large flowers with diameters of four inches or more. Tuberous begonias usually produce one male bud flanked by two female buds on a flowering stem. The male bud is the bloom; therefore, the females buds are removed. Upright begonias become quite tall, so careful staking is needed.

PENDULA BEGONIAS

Among the hanging basket displays there is often a collection of pendula begonias, a cascading long stemmed begonia. To shape a pendula begonia, the growing tip is pinched back after four inches of growth. This allows for new side shoots or laterals to develop. With this type of begonia it is not necessary to remove the female buds.

FINDING THE RIGHT LOCATION

When planting or finding a good location for begonias, one must keep in mind that the leaves point to the front, and the flower also faces in that direction. Begonias are generally known as shade-loving plants, but they also seem to benefit from the early morning or late afternoon sun. Mildew on begonia leaves is caused by a lack of air circulation. When this occurs, the affected leaves must be removed and the plant relocated.

WATERING AND FEEDING

A cautious watering and feeding program is applied to begonias. The plants are watered only when the surface of the soil has become dry. Overwatering causes the buds to drop off. A light feeding of 10-52-17 can be given after several sets of true leaves have formed. As the plants show a continual growth, a frequent but light feeding of 20-20-20 or fish fertilizer can be applied. If begonias are over-fed, the edges of the leaves will curl under.

PREPARING FOR WINTER

As the summer begins to draw to an end, the watering decreases, and the plant leaves start turning yellow. This is the time to withhold watering so that the stem will dry up and drop off. A light frost speeds up this process and blackens the begonia stems and leaves. They should be immediately lifted from the garden or containers. The blackened tops are removed, and the tubers are washed and left to dry. Once the tuber is dry, it should be dusted well with powdered sulphur. For winter storage, the tubers should be placed in a box and covered with dry peat. Like other bulbs they are stored in a cool frost-free area.

HANGING BASKETS

It is rewarding to make a hanging basket from the cuttings and seedlings grown in a greenhouse. The best time to make a hanging basket is six weeks before the basket is ready to go outside. At that time, the cuttings and seedlings have become sizeable plants. Hanging baskets prefer a night temperature of 10°C (50°F) and a day temperature of about 18°C (65°F).

THE BASKET

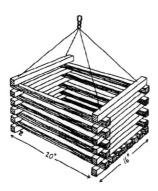

Plastic baskets have been in use for a long time and have a water tray attached to the bottom of the basket. One must always check that the basket has large enough drainage holes; one can even add a few extra holes. Wire baskets are lined with moss which helps to retain the moisture. Moss can be purchased in bags, or if one lives in a high rainfall area, the moss can be collected from trees. Wooden lattice baskets are also moss lined and not difficult to construct. I have found that compressed peat hanging baskets will dry out very quickly, especially if there is a slight bit of wind.

SOIL MIX

Soils for hanging baskets require a higher peat content to help retain moisture. A well proven mix is one part sterilized soil, two parts peat, and one-half part perlite or sand. The prepared soilless mixes available at the garden centres are also a good choice for hanging baskets.

PLANT SELECTION FOR HANGING BASKETS

Baskets of geraniums and fuchsias are old favorites because they are not difficult to make and will bloom continually all summer. The centre of the basket needs an upright variety, with a selection of trailing plants cascading over the sides. Petunias and impatiens also make colourful displays in hanging baskets. Creating mixed baskets of cuttings, seedlings and foliage is an art and requires some plant knowledge. All the plants selected must be compatible with the chosen location, whether in the sun or in the shade. Plant selection is a mix of early and late flowering plants so that the basket will have continuous blooms all season.

A basket of ivy geraniums

Some other plants for hanging baskets are fibrous begonias, coleus, blue marguerite, viscaria, heliotrope, lotus vine, potato vine, trailing verbena, nepeta, black-eyed susan vine, lobelia, schizanthus, vinca or periwinkle, browallia, dwarf tagetes, marigold and ivy.

TRANSPLANTING

Plants should be selected that are well rooted and show good leaf growth. These include the seedlings previously transplanted in four-inch pots.The plants are placed so close together that the roots touch each other. Upright plants should be placed in the middle, and trailing plants and foliage along the outside edge of the basket. Transplanting still creates a shock, and roots need to re-establish in a larger container. A few diluted feedings of 10-52-17 root builder give them a good start. To ensure that the plants are growing symmetrically, the baskets need to be turned frequently.

LOCATION FOR HANGING BASKETS

Geraniums and petunias need the full sun, while begonias, fuchsias and impatiens prefer the shade. The greenhouse has shading, and one must provide adequate ventilation and circulation.Suspending the baskets from the roof bars of the greenhouse gives the baskets the best light conditions. It also makes sure there is room for trailing plants to grow. Hanging baskets need protection from wind or excessive rain, so the most suitable location outside the greenhouse is under the overhang of the house.

WATERING, FEEDING AND PLANT CARE

It takes time to care for hanging baskets. How often one waters depends on the temperature and exposure to sun. During the spring, while the baskets are in the greenhouse, one's daily observation is the guide to watering. In the greenhouse on sunny days, the hanging baskets can become dry very quickly. The best method of watering

35

is a good soaking so that the water runs out of the bottom of the baskets.

The first feeding for hanging baskets is a diluted measure of 10-52-17 for building up the roots. When the roots are established, active growth becomes evident and diluted feedings of 20-20-20 can then begin. Once the baskets are moved outside, the watering becomes daily, and diluted feedings of 20-20-20 can be given as often as every other day in the middle of the summer. Since plants grow very quickly in the summer months, I replace some feedings with 10-52-17 so that the roots can develop as quickly as the top growth.

For the plants to remain healthy and free from disease, any dead leaves should be removed from the baskets.

As the season progresses, all flowers that have finished blooming must be removed, a process called "deadheading". However, the plants will continue to produce new flowers.

A mixed hanging basket of geraniums, verbena, lotus vine and ivy.

CHAPTER

Eight

GREENHOUSE VEGETABLES

Most greenhouse gardeners enjoy the advantage of being able to start the season early and also to extend it, but they find that year round vegetable growing is just too costly. In areas where the growing season is short or unpredictable, plants kept in the greenhouse guarantees a vegetable crop.

STARTING VEGETABLES FOR THE GARDEN

January is the month for planning for the upcoming season in the greenhouse and in the garden. In January, one usually selects seeds for outdoor vegetables and greenhouse crops. In some areas, seed sowing for garden crops can be started in the greenhouse as early as February. In areas where frost is not expected until late fall, a second crop of hardy vegetables can be sown in June for harvesting in late fall.

GREENHOUSE VEGETABLE CROPS

Crops of tomatoes and cucumbers are the first vegetables that come to the mind of a greenhouse gardener. In a cool greenhouse, the earliest date for sowing tomato seeds is March, and for cucumbers, April. I have found that sowing both crops on April lst has been very successful, and the crops can still being harvested in October. For the cooler climates, the seeds should be sown one month later. Some heating is still necessary in the cooler climates since the ideal minimum night temperature for these plants is 13°C (55°F).

TOMATOES

When the seedlings have developed their first set of leaves, they can be transplanted into 4" pots with sterilized potting soil.

Transplanting tomato plants to a permanent location, in larger pots or raised soil beds, is done when the plants have developed their first truss with one flower.

Growing tomato plants in five-gallon black plastic pots has been successful in my greenhouse. I add a few extra drainage holes to the bottom of the pot, and then place it on a bed of gravel. The plants have ample space as the roots continue to grow into the gravel bed. Tomato plants are secured against a wooden or bamboo stake and tied securely with a strong rope.

The tomato plants prefer daily water, but the amount of water should be regulated according to the weather and temperature. The amount of water can vary from one cup on dull cloudy days to half a gallon on sunny days. During the summer months, the watering increases to twice a day. Feeding starts to take place after flowering and after the fruit begins to form. Liquid tomato fertilizer is high in phosphate and potash, nutrients which encourage fruit development and sustain root formation. The application of liquid fertilizer is recommended once a week, but, if one dilutes the feeding, the fertilizer can be applied every few days.

Small shoots grow just above the leaf joints. These are commonly known as suckers and will take plant energy from the main truss. Therefore, the suckers should be removed as soon as they become visible.

Tomato plants at a certain stage of growth need some control, or they will take over the greenhouse. When the plant has reached the height of the greenhouse or has at least seven trusses set, the growing tip can be pinched out. To help with pollination for fruit-bearing plants, the support stakes should be tapped daily.

Early October is normally the end of the growing season for tomatoes.

CUCUMBERS

Varieties of seeds of long English cucumbers typically produce the best growing cucumber in a greenhouse environment. The traditional cucumber plants has male and female flowers, and the male flower had to be removed. The new varieties have only female flowers and are more disease resistant. Self-pollinating varieties save the time of tapping the stakes or strings each day to help pollination.

Cucumber seeds quickly germinate in two or three days on a propagating bed. Since the seeds are large and easy to handle, they can be started directly in four-inch peat pots. Tranplanting to five-gallon pots or grow bags is required when two sets of true leaves have formed.

Varieties of cucumbers that have the male and female flowers bear fruit on the side shoots of the plant. Male flowers and non-flowering side shoots are removed from the cucumber plant. With all female varieties the main stem bears the fruit, and all side shoots are removed.

Staking the cucumber vine can be done like the tomato plants by using a wooden or bamboo stake. Another method is to train the cucumber plants to grow up along twine strings that are fastened to the roof bars. When the plants have grown about five feet, they can be trained to continue growing along the eaves.

Cucumbers prefer small doses of water which must be applied frequently. However, one must be very cautious not to overwater the plants.

Frequent watering can be controlled with an automatic timed watering system. Diluted liquid tomato fertilizer is fed to the plants once the fruits have formed.

Early October is also the end of the growing season for cucumbers in the greenhouse.

GREENHOUSE ENVIRONMENT

Fluctuating temperatures in the greenhouse is a major cause of plant or crop damage. This can be controlled by adequate air circulation, ventilation and shading. During the summer months, a regular "damping down" of the greenhouse increases the humidity level and cools the air. "Damping down" is discussed under "Humidity" in chapter six.

Tomato and cucumber plants are very susceptible to drawing whitefly. To prevent a serious infestation, one can hang a few yellow whitefly strips around each plant. Any yellow or discoloured leaves should also be removed from the plants.

LETTUCE AND RADISHES

Once the tomatoes and cucumbers have vacated the greenhouse, a winter crop of lettuce can start to fill the space. Maximum light conditions are required for lettuce, and in areas where natural light is limited, artificial lighting is needed. Like other growing vegetables, twelve hours of light is the minimum requirement. In the Pacific coastal regions, seeds sown in early September have a crop in early November, and no extra light is needed. At the end of October, the days become shorter; newly started lettuce seedlings need a few additional hours of artificial light. Fast growing winter lettuce seeds provide the most successful crops. Seeds are started on a propagating bed and transplanted into seedling inserts which are placed on the bench. Once the roots have been established, they are transplanted into soil beds at ground level. I put my portable two-foot summer planters to good use when growing winter lettuce in the greenhouse. Each planter holds six to eight lettuce plants, depending on the variety.

Radishes are quick growing plants which need very little room. These can be directly sown between the lettuce plants.

Lettuce and radishes, which are grown in cool temperatures, only need a little watering every few days. This will again depend on the greenhouse temperature during the day.

HERBS

Chives, parsley, mint, rosemary, sage and thyme are herbs that can be brought in from the garden to be wintered over in the greenhouse. They can be potted in clumps and given a little water on a regular basis. Some of the leaves will die from the transplant and need to be removed to keep the plant healthy. Herbs can also be started from seeds and grown in a cool greenhouse.

Early varieties of potatoes and carrots are other vegetables to try in a cool greenhouse. January is the planting time for the spring crop, and September for the winter crops.

CHAPTER

Nine

CACTI AND ORCHIDS

The more involved one becomes with greenhouse gardening, the more he or she wants to experiment with a wider selection of plants. Greenhouse plant collections often start with a cutting from a friend's plant or a package of seeds picked up while travelling. The distinctive flowers of orchids and cacti quickly catch the attention of the greenhouse gardener. These plants are not difficult to grow, and some of their species are adaptable to the cool greenhouse conditions.

CACTI

Desert cacti are unique plants that can adapt to the summer's heat and the winter's cold and can still produce flowers.

The natural habitat of the cacti is very dry, and the crushed rock desert soil is not very fertile. The temperatures fluctuate from very high during the day to close to freezing at night. A seasonal, irregular rainfall forces the cacti to bloom. Greenhouse cacti often fail to bloom because they are carefully nurtured just like the other plants. As soon as one neglects the cacti and does very little watering, the plants begin to flower.

SEEDS

Local garden centres carry cactus seeds in the speciality seed section. Seeds are sown in early spring. In late August they are mature enough to be transplanted. Cacti seeds are small, so they

A flowering cacti display surrounded with impatiens

must be mixed with some sand. Seeds can be sprinkled into a shallow container of sterilized seedling mix and covered with a light layer of soil. They prefer a bottom watering from a water bath. Bottom heat from a soil cable improves the cacti's chances of success. To retain the heat and humidity, the container can be covered with a sheet of glass or clear plastic.The germination period for cacti seeds ranges from three to ten weeks. To prevent the soil from drying during these weeks, a light misting of water can be applied.

Once the cacti seeds have germinated, the glass or plastic cover is removed a few hours a day at the start, and this time period is lengthened slowly until the seedlings are ready for transplanting. Transplanted cacti are treated as mature plants, but at this early stage they are not yet adaptable to cooler temperatures. In a cool greenhouse, these plants should be placed in the warmest location or given some bottom heat from the soil cable at night.

Mature cacti multiply by producing an abundance of side shoots or "offsets" at the base of the plant. These shoots can be removed for individual plants, but the base of the new shoots must be allowed to dry before repotting.

TRANSPLANTING

Pre-mixed cacti soil from the garden centre is a coarse mix, consisting of crushed gravel, sand and bricks, for proper drainage. Cacti offsets, or seedlings, are transplanted into small pots and left in these containers until they are quite root bound. Repotting to permanent pots is done when the roots are well developed and active growth is evident. Care must be taken to cut away any dead roots before transplanting or repotting.

LOCATION

Desert cacti should be located on the bench in full sunlight, but in the summer months some shading is needed to protect them from sunburn. Overheating in the summer can cause cacti damage, so the greenhouse must have adequate ventilation. Cacti are very adaptable, but the greenhouse temperature must not fall below freezing. Some desert cacti are capable of becoming large plants. Therefore, a permanent location for these plants should be a coarse sand and crushed gravel bed at ground level. This location must have full exposure to sunlight.

WATERING

Whenever it rains in the desert, cacti start to bloom. For the greenhouse cacti, the watering is done so that the plant blooms in the summer. No watering is required from October to March. The forced heat in the greenhouse can cause the cacti to show signs of shrivelling, in which case a very light misting can be made on the cacti. In the spring, the cacti start to have a growing spurt. At this time, a little watering can be applied. As the flower buds form, watering is done once or twice a week depending on the amount of sun the plant is exposed to. Cacti in my greenhouse seem to have their own flowering cycles from early summer to fall, but never all at the same time. Some cacti have a very short flowering period of only one day. After flowering, the watering is again slowly decreased.

Christmas cacti are taken out of the greenhouse during the summer months and placed in a shady area of the garden. September and October are the cool and dry periods, and in November the Christmas cacti are watered twice a week. After the cacti have finished flowering, the watering can begin to be decreased.

ORCHIDS

Once the bloom of one orchid is enjoyed for several months, often it leads to the purchase of a few more orchid plants. Orchids are a speciality plant, but they can spark the interest of some gardeners so much that the greenhouse is transformed into a climatized orchid house.

Like cacti, the climatic conditions of the natural habitat of the orchid must be recreated in the greenhouse. Many of the plants discussed in this book have definite summer and winter seasons, but the orchid is somewhat different. Some orchids do not adapt well to more than a 20-25 degree Fahrenheit temperature difference between night and day. This is especially true over long periods of time. Growing a cool orchid in the greenhouse requires a *cool atmosphere year-round.*

If one has a few cool orchids in a greenhouse in the winter, they should be brought into the house during the spring and summer. The best location is a light kitchen or bathroom so that the plants still have the needed humidity. For the best results, the climatic conditions and plant care should be requested when an orchid plant is purchased.

GREENHOUSE TEMPERATURES

The most common orchids can be grown in three different temperature greenhouses. Orchids are able to withstand a lower recommended temperature by 5 degrees Fahrenheit, but if cooler conditions remain constant, botrytis or soft rot can affect the plants.

Cymbidium Orchid

COOL: Night temperature
7°C (45°F)
(odontoglossum and laelia)

INTERMEDIATE: Night temperature
10°C (50°F)to 16°C (60°F)
(cymbidium and cattleya)

WARM: Night temperature
16°C (60°F) to 20°C (70°F)
(Dendrobium and phalaenopsis)

OTHER CLIMATIC CONDITIONS

During the spring and summer, the greenhouse is dependent on intake louvres, exhaust fans and circulating fans in order to control the temperature. Depending on the orchid, either shading or full light conditions are required. One orchid greenhouse that I visited on the West Coast required no extra lighting in the warm greenhouse. However, when there is insufficient daylight, growlights must be added. In the warmer greenhouses, the humidity levels are high, and a small humidifier helps to maintain this level. Gravel floors can also be sprayed in order to create more humidity in the greenhouse.

ORCHID POTTING MIX

Bark is the base ingredient of the orchid mix, and with additions of peat moss, perlite and unusual material like styrofoam, an open, aerated and well draining mix is created. Orchid bark, like other potting soils, is also heat treated. For a few orchids, a prepared orchid mix is available at the garden centres. Since bark becomes very dry, it should be drenched with boiling water before the orchids are potted.

WATERING AND FEEDING

Watering and feeding requirements are different for each variety

47

of orchid. It is difficult to tell whether the mix is dry, so one method is to lift the pot, and if it is heavy no water is needed. A light weight pot requires watering. Cool orchids in the greenhouse probably need very little water during the winter season, and, in the spring when they bloom, frequent watering and feeding is done. Feeding orchids is very similar to other plants: very diluted feedings can be applied with each watering. A well-balanced orchid fertilizer, like Dyna Grow, with ingredients of calcium and magnesium is distributed through Valley Orchid Partners in Pitt Meadows, B.C.

PEST CONTROL

Pests such as whitefly and aphids are also present in orchid greenhouses. The whitefly does not seem to bother the plant leaves, and yellow glue traps keep whiteflies under control. Aphids can do damage to some species, but daily observation prevents an infestation. One orchid grower gave me a few interesting tips to control pests and diseases with the use of a few household products. Isopropyl alcohol can be lightly rubbed on the infested area to eliminate any pests on the plant. Cinnamon sprinkled on the leaves is very effective against fungal diseases. The infected plant must always be isolated until there is no further sign of any pests. Some other preventative measures in the greenhouse include sterilized potting mixes, the use of clean pots and the removal of old leaves from the growing area. Although the humidity level may be high, constant air movement and ventilation is also a deterrent to pests.

CHAPTER

Ten

COLDFRAMES

Coldframes provide the welcome additional space that the greenhouse gardener needs, especially in the early spring. An average coldframe covers 1.1 to 1.4 m² (12-16 ft²). Coldframes can be constructed from wood or aluminum framing, with glass pane, plastic or polycarbonate coverings. Sliding or hinged lids provide adequate ventilation during the day, and they can be closed for protection against cooler temperatures at night. These lids slope so that rain and snow run off. Greenhouse suppliers carry prefabricated coldframes that are light weight so that they can be dismantled or moved from one location to another.

Like a greenhouse, the coldframe needs some shade protection for the plants in spring and summer. In cooler climates, the coldframe must be insulated for winter use.

COLDFRAME PLANTS

In an area where no heavy frosts are expected, the coldframes give enough protection to winter over tender garden plants. It is recommended that a soil cable be installed in the coldframe. Weather conditions are often unpredictable, and a soil cable gives enough warmth to keep the frost off the plants.

Early crops of garden vegetables are taken from the greenhouse and stored in the coldframe. Here they become acclimatized or go through the "hardening off" period. As well, vegetable seedlings can be planted directly into the coldframe soil bed.

If the coldframe is not in use by the beginning of May, the bedding plants can be transferred from the greenhouse to the frame so that they can become acclimitized before being planted in the garden. This area provides the necessary protection from the cool temperatures at night.

From September to November, if the coldframe is not used for late vegetable crops, it can be an ideal location for bulb forcing. Bulbs that have been pre-treated for forcing still need to go through at least a ten-week period of darkness known as the "plunging" period. Low temperatures ensure that the roots become established, but the temperatures should be no lower than 5°C (40°F). The potted bulbs are placed in the coldframe, and for added frost protection they are covered with four inches of moist peat. Being protected from all the elements, the peat needs to be watered occasionally so that the bulbs do not dry out. The bulbs should be checked regularly near the end of November, and once two or three inches of the bulbs is showing, the pots can be lifted and placed in a shady spot under the bench in the greenhouse. A seven-day period of shade is needed for stems to develop. Then they can be moved to full light on the bench and kept moist. By Christmas, the greenhouse will have a display of flowering hyacinths, tulips and narcissi.

A winter display of hyacinth bulbs

CHAPTER

Eleven

PREVENTION OF GREENHOUSE
PESTS AND DISEASES

GREENHOUSE STRUCTURE

Prevention is the best known method of controlling pests and diseases in the greenhouse. During the summer months, pests find the greenhouse conditions very suitable for breeding. Once a year the greenhouse needs to be washed down inside and out. This task should be undertaken when the greenhouse has the least number of plants, generally just before the garden plants are brought in for wintering over. A recommended cleaning solution is a mixture of hot water and a disinfectant of Lysol, Pinesol or household bleach. Benches, shelving, plastic trays, pots and baskets should also be cleaned thoroughly.

If not controlled, the greenhouse air can become dry and stale; spider mites, mealy bugs and earwigs will thrive in this atmosphere. When the humidity level is very high, pests like the whitefly and diseases like powdery mildew and moulds become a problem. Constant air movement from a circulating fan, and adequate ventilation help provide a pest-and disease-free environment.

PLANTS

Aphids and whiteflies are common pests associated with garden plants. To eliminate the possibility of plants being the carriers of these pests, each plant brought into the greenhouse needs to be washed down with soapy water. Bar soap or safer insecticide soap should be used, not detergent.

Checking plants regularly leads to early visual detection of problems like moulds, mildew and leaf discoloration. Any infested leaves should be removed, and the plant should be washed and placed in isolation for a few days. At this time, one can tell if the problem is under control. In some cases, it is better to dispose of the diseased plant.

It is natural for old leaves to die off when new leaves appear. Quick removal of dead leaves from benches, floors and shelving prevents a breeding area for pests.

Fuchsias, geraniums, cucumbers and tomatoes are plants that are very susceptible to the white fly. An old fashioned but effective controlling device is to burn a mosquito coil. Once lit, the coil releases fumes that are very effective against the whitefly. A few years ago, I tested several brands of yellow sticky strips and found that the non toxic horti-kure strip provided the best results. The strips are hung close to the plants, and for larger plants like cucumbers several strips are used. Regular sprayings of safer soap also prevent an outbreak of whitefly and other pests.

SOILS
There is nothing more disappointing for the gardener than to find his or her seedlings wilting and disappearing overnight. This condition is called "damping off," a disease that can be prevented by using sterilized soil and by carefully watering the seedlings.

Cuttings can have a similar "damping off" problem that appears as "root rot," in which the base of the cutting turns black. Again, sterilized soil and careful watering are the necessary preventative measures.

Keeping the soil too dry causes the buds of healthy plants to wither or drop off. This problem can be eliminated if the soil is kept moist while the bud is forming.

INSECTICIDE SPRAYS
At times, one can use all the preventative measures including constant ventilation and circulation of the air in the greenhouse,

yet still find an infestation of pests or disease. Insecticides are constantly being improved, and the experts at the garden centres know which insecticide is best for each particular greenhouse pest. It is wise to use the products exactly as specified on the manufacturer's label. An increased application can cause irreversible plant damage.

CHAPTER
Twelve

THE ONE YEAR
COOL GREENHOUSE CALENDAR

JANUARY

PLANTS:
- Sow slow-growing seeds, like fibrous begonias and geraniums.
- Using a large deep pots, start seed potatoes.
- Sow early varieties of carrots in soil beds or deep planters.
- Bring in the bulbs for flowering which have wintered in the coldframe since October.
- Prune the climbers like the bougainvilla or passion flower for spring growth.
- In the warmer climates, start last year's tuberous begonias on the propagating bed if they showing growth.

GREENHOUSE:
- Ventilate the greenhouse on sunny days, and daily check and record the night temperatures.
- Continue checking for pests or diseases.
- Sterilize soil to prepare for the upcoming planting season.
- Send in seed orders from catalogues.

FEBRUARY

PLANTS:
- Sow the early bedding plants and garden vegetables according to the seedling charts.
- Start early lettuce, but additional lighting may still be required.

55

- Purchase and start begonia tuber.
- Repotting may be necessary for some of the plants that have wintered over and are showing active growth.
- Clivias may bloom and will require regular watering.
- Water seedlings when necessary for seedlings, but be careful not to overwater.

GREENHOUSE:
- Continue ventilation on sunny days.
- Maintain adequate air circulation to prevent condensation.

MARCH

PLANTS:
- Sow the remaining bedding plants and early garden vegetable seeds.
- Seedlings planted in the previous months are ready for transplanting.
- Begonias tubers are ready for transplanting; in the cooler climates the tubers can be started.
- Take additional spring cuttings from the fuchsias and geraniums.
- If you are planning to grow winter flowering pot plants like cinneria, gloxinia or cyclamen, sow them in early spring because they are slow growing. Follow the seed catalogue planting information for each variety of pot plant.
- Increase watering and feeding for the overwintered plants. Overwatering the seedlings can cause "damping off".

GREENHOUSE:
- Provide some shading for protecting the young seedlings.
- Early spring can be unpredictable, but usually there are more sunny days and the greenhouse vents are opened more frequently. You can now activate the automatic vent opener .

APRIL

PLANTS:
- Transplant into four-inch pots the cuttings taken in March. Also transplant into permanent containers the cuttings that are to remain in the greenhouse as pot plants.
- Tranplant the bedding plants.
- Now comes the final sowing of seeds for the garden vegetables: bring the vegetables seedlings into the coldframe to "harden off" or directly plant the seedlings into the coldframe.
- Sow the greenhouse cucumbers and tomatoes on April lst.
- Make hanging baskets from the cuttings and well potted seedlings.
- Pinch back the begonias, fuchsias, geraniums and other seedlings.
- Start watering the cacti.
- Slowly increase the watering and feeding of all plants.

GREENHOUSE:
- For the hanging baskets, maintain the night temperature is at 10°C (50°F).
- Remove greenhouse insulation and put up shading material.
- Check daily for pests and diseases.
- Open vents and louvres for longer periods of time, and near the end of the month open them at all times, but watch for drafts.
- Check and record daytime readings on the maximum-minimum thermometer.
- As the outside temperature increases, use the greenhouse heater only minimally.

MAY

PLANTS:
- Transplant tomatoes and cucumbers to final containers.
- Harvest greenhouse lettuce, potatoes and carrots.
- Move bedding plants to the cold frames or protected areas outside to "harden off".
- Plant garden vegetables seedlings early in the month.

- Place the hanging baskets in protected areas, or let them remain in the greenhouse until the last week of May. If they remain in the greenhouse, leave open the doors and vents to acclimitize the baskets.
- Check the watering needs of the plants daily.
- Move cool orchids into the house.

GREENHOUSE:
- In the milder climates, discontinue the heating (in the cooler climates night heat may still be necessary).
- Check and record the day temperature of the greenhouse for adequate venting and circulating.

JUNE

PLANTS:
- Water and regularly feed tomatoes and cucumbers. Stake the plants. Tap the stakes daily for pollination.
- Cacti respond to a slight increase of watering.
- Store the Christmas cactus pots in a shaded garden area.

GREENHOUSE:
- On hot days, "damp down" the greenhouse to increase the humidity and cool down the atmosphere.
- Clean and store any portable heaters.
- Continue to check and record the daytime temperature.
- Remove and store the automatic vent opener cylinder for the summer months..

JULY

PLANTS:
- Cacti and bromeliads start to bloom.
- Begin to harvest cucumbers and tomatoes.
- House plants enjoy the humidity of the greenhouse during the summer months.
- Continue watering and feeding tomatoes and cucumbers.

- Continually water and feed the annual plants kept in the greenhouse for summer display.

GREENHOUSE:
- "Damp down" the greenhouse daily.
- Watch closely for pests and diseases.
- Day temperature can become too high if there is not enough air circulation. Install an extra circulating fan or exhaust fan, if necessary

AUGUST
PLANTS:
- Take cuttings from the garden's best plants, like coleus, fuchsias, geraniums and impatiens.
- Place cutting trays on the greenhouse bench with no bottom heat. Keep cuttings moist.
- Continually pick tomato and cucumber crops.
- Transplant cinneria, cyclamen and gloxina plants into permanent containers.
- Water and feed all plants daily, and continue to "damp down" the greenhouse.

GREENHOUSE:
- Tap tomato and cucumber stakes to pollinate the plants for September's crop.
- At the end of the month, re-install the cylinder to the automatic vent opener.

SEPTEMBER
PLANTS:
- Transplant cuttings taken in August into 4" pots.
- Take new cuttings, but they require bottom heat.
- Place containers of forcing bulbs in the coldframe or the storage shed, to be brought in later for winter flowering.
- Sow winter lettuce crop. Start another pot of potatoes under

the bench.

- In the cooler climates, bring in frost sensitive plants to be wintered over.
- Place cool orchids in the greenhouse again.
- Decrease watering and feeding for outside and greenhouse plants in preparation for winter.

GREENHOUSE:
- *In the cooler climates*, give the greenhouse its annual cleaning.
- Remove shading and put up greenhouse insulation.
- Remove greenhouse tomatoes and cucumbers.
- Use heating equipment for the cooler nights.
- In the milder climates the plants are still in full bloom; keep them outside as long as possible.

OCTOBER

PLANTS:
- Cut back frost sensitive plants and bring them in for overwinteri
- Cut back and keep the parent plants from which the summer and fall cuttings were taken.
- Bring in the tuberous begonias after the first frost.
- Stop watering the cacti plants.
- Plant more containers of forcing bulbs for January and February blooms.
- At the end of the month, transplant cuttings taken in September.

GREENHOUSE:
- Store the automatic vent opener cylinder for the winter season.
- Control the venting manually on warm days.
- Make sure the air circulation is adequate in order to prevent condensation.
- In the latter part of October, use heating units for the cooler nights.
- *In the warmer climates*, the tomato and cucumber season has come to an end.

- Remove and store shading material.
- Do annual greenhouse cleaning and install insulation.

NOVEMBER

PLANTS:
- Transplant the remaining geranium and fuchsia cuttings.
- Cut the outer lettuce leaves for salads.
- Water only when the plant needs it, since many plants are now in the dormant stage.
- Start watering the Christmas cacti, and the flower buds will start to form.
- Keep the plants clean by removing any discoloured or dying leaves.
- Water the bulbs in the coldframe to prevent the bulbs from drying out.
- Carefully water cyclamen, cinneria and gloxina plants.

GREENHOUSE:
- Continue to ventilate during sunny days.
- Provide constant air circulation.
- Check and record the night temperatures every 24 hours.

DECEMBER

PLANTS:
- Bring in the bulbs for Christmas flowering.
- Sparingly water the Christmas cactus, cinneria, cyclamen and gloxina.
- Lightly mist the cacti to prevent any shrivelling of the leaves.
- Pinch back any cuttings that may form flower buds.
- Lift the potatoes, and harvest the lettuce crop.

GREENHOUSE:
- Very cold spells can occur this month, so keep a close watch on night temperatures, and set the heaters accordingly.
- Use venting when the weather permits; even prop open the vent

with a thin piece of wood to bring some fresh air into the greenhouse atmosphere.
- When the cool greenhouse has some flowering plants during
  the winter, watering these plants to increase the condensation
  inside. Air circulation and ventilation is necessary.
- Write for seed catalogues so that the seeds can be ordered
  in January.

A bed of summer marigolds started with spring seed
propagation in the greenhouse.

CHAPTER

Thirteen

PLANT REFERENCE CHARTS

SEEDING CHART

Plant Variety	Month to Sow
ageratum	February
alyssum	March
aster	March
balsam	March
begonia fibrous	January
browallia	March **
black-eyed Susan	February **
calceolaria	March **
calendula	February
coleus	March **
carnation	February **
dahlia	March
dianthus	March
geranium	January **
godetia	March
heliothrope	February
impatiens	March
lobelia	February
marigold	March
nasturtium	March
nemesia	March
nicotina	March
petunia	March
phlox	March
portulaca	March
primula	February **
snapdragon	February
salvia	March
schizanthus	March
verbena	March
viscaria	March
zinnia	March

**These seedlings can be potted and remain in the greenhouse as flowering display plants.

VEGETABLE SEEDING CHART

Plant Variety	Month to Sow
asparagus	April
beet	March
broccoli	March
Brussel sprouts	April
cabbage	February
cauliflower	March
celery	February
cucumber	April
leek	February
lettuce	February
onion	February
pepper	March
pumpkin	April
squash	April
spinach	February
tomato	April

CUTTING CHART

Plant Variety	Cutting Time	Night Temperature	
azalea	after flowering	45° F	7°C
coleus	summer in water	50° F	10°C
camellia	summer	45° F	7°C
flowering maple	spring	45° F	7°C
fibrous begonia	spring	50° F	10°C
impatiens	summer in water	50° F	10°C
geranium	summer/spring	40-45° F	5-7°C
fuchsias	summer/spring	40- 45°F	5-7°C
marguariete daisy	summer	45° F	7°C
gazanias .	summer	50° F	10°C
heliotrope	summer	50° F	10°C
lantana	summer	45° F	7°C

GREENHOUSE POTTED PLANTS

Plant Variety	Propagation	Night temperature	
abutilon	seed/cutting	45° F	7° C
African violet	leaf cutting	60° F	16° C
azalea	cuttings	45° F	7° C
bromeliad	offsets	45° F	7° C
coleus	cutting/seed	50° F	10° C
calceolaria	seeds	45° F	7° C
camellia	cuttings	45° F	7° C
clivia	offsets	50° F	10° C
cyclamen	corm/seeds	50° F	10° C
carnation	seeds	45° F	7° C
cinneraria	seeds	45° F	7° C
cactus	seeds/offsets	45° F	7° C
gloxinia	seeds	50° F	10° C
kalanchoe	seeds	50° F	7° C
primula	seeds	45° F	7° C
streptocarpus	leaf cutting	50° F	10° C

CLIMBERS AND STANDARDS

Plant Variety	Plant Care	Night Temperature	
bougainvillea	winter pruning	45° F	7° C
hoya	drier in winter	45° F	7° C
hibiscus	winter pruning	50° F	10° C
fuchsia tree	fall pruning	45° F	10° C
lantana tree	fall pruning	45° F	10° C
passionflower	winter pruning	45° F	7° C
polyanthum jasmine	winter pruning	45° F	7° C
fern	drier in winter	45° F	7° C

CHAPTER
Fourteen

SOURCES OF INFORMATION

RECORDKEEPING

The notes that are kept in a journal become the best source of information for greenhouse gardening. Not only do they show gardening accomplishments, but they also provide information on any difficulties that are encountered. Here are a few examples of recorded information for successful greenhouse gardening.

DAILY TEMPERATURE RECORD

Recorded temperatures inside the greenhouse determine whether the heater thermostat is accurate, and the ventilation adequate.

DAILY TEMPERATURE RECORD

Date	Night Temp.	Day Temp.

PLANTING RECORD

Recording the dates and results of seedlings, cuttings and bulb planting helps in the next year's greenhouse planning.

SEED/CUTTINGS/BULB RECORD

Date	Planting	Results

PLANT FEEDING RECORD

It is often difficult to remember on which day the plants were fed and which fertilizer was used. Recording this information prevents irregular or overfeeding of the plants.

RECORD OF PLANT FEEDING

Date	Fertilizer	Amount Applied

Notations of unusual plants and trial experiments complete the reference book.

SEED CATALOGUES

Once a year, new seed catalogues are printed with the numerous seeds and plants available for the upcoming year. The catalogues not only sell seeds but also provide valuable information on germination, maturity and disease-resistant seeds. Many catalogues have an indoor plant section which lists the seeds for greenhouse gardening.

Stokes Seeds Ltd.
P.O. Box 10,
St. Catharines, Ontario, L2R 6R6
Dominion Seed House
Georgetown, Ontario, L7G 4A2
William Dam Seeds
P.O. Box 8400,
Dundas, Ontario, L9H 6M1
Thompson & Morgan
P.O. Box 1308,
Jackson, New Jersey, U.S.A. 08527
T & T Seeds
P.O. Box 1710,
Winnipeg, Manitoba, R3C 3P6

REGIONAL SEED COMPANIES

Alberta Nurseries and Seeds
Bowden, Alberta, TOM OKO
Butchart Gardens
P.O. Box 4010, Station "A"
Victoria, B.C., V8X 3X4
Pacific Northwest Seed
P.O Box 460
Vernon, B.C., V1T 6M4
Territorial Seeds (Canada)
#206-8475 Ontario Street,
Vancouver, B.C. V5X 3E8
Territorial Seed Company,
P.O. Box 27,
Lorane, Oregon, USA 97451

GARDENING BOOKS

Greenhouse gardening is often just the beginning of a plant's lifecycle. Once the plants are planted in the garden and the hanging baskets are hung outdoors, the care of the plants changes. These selected books provide further gardening information on the plants discussed in this book:

A Year in Your Garden, written by David Tarrant, the well-known T.V. host of " The Canadian Gardener," is published by Whitecap Books and is available in most bookstores. This book is a month-by-month guide to gardening in British Columbia. Hanging baskets, annuals and vegetables are just a few of the topics covered in this book.

The Complete Guide to Bedding Plants For Amateurs and Experts, written by Carolyn Jones and published by Whitecap books, is available in most bookstores. The colour pictures and the encyclopedic indexing of bedding plants makes this book a handy reference manual.

How to Grow Fuchsias and Begonias, is written and published by The B.C. Fuchsia and Begonia Society, c/o Lorna Herchenson, 2402 Swinburne, North Vancouver, B.C. V7H 1L2. This little booklet is a valuable addition to a gardener's library. It starts with the history of fuchsias and begonias, followed by detailed instructions from propagation right through to winter storage.

Your First Orchids and How to Grow Them, a publication of the Oregon Orchid Society Inc., is available through the Orchid Society P.O. Box 14182, Portland, Oregon, 96214. It is also available through Valley Orchid Partners, 12621 Woolridge Road, Pitt Meadows, B.C., V3Y 1Z1. This is a handy reference book and beginner's guide to commonly grown orchids. Each orchid species is discussed in detail with reference to plant care and the greenhouse environment.

Sunset Western Garden Book, published by Sunset Publication Corporation, is available in most bookstores. The alphabetical plant encyclopedia provides easy reference for most gardener's needs.

Hanging Baskets of Victoria, B.C., ia a video produced by the renowned gardener Brian Minter. It is available through MetroMedia, #1-228 Edward Street, Victoria, B.C., V9A 3E5. This video, suitable for gardeners of all levels, helps anyone make incredible hanging baskets.

GARDEN CLUBS

Garden clubs meet on a regular basis to share information on selected plants. The most popular clubs are the fuchsia, begonia, geranium, cactus and orchid societies. Local newspapers also provide information about local clubs under their weekly calendar of events. For further information on clubs and gardening courses in your area, contact the local universities.

University of British Columbia
Botanical Gardens "Hortline" (garden club information)
6804 S.W. Marine Dr., Vancouver, B.C. V6T 1Z4
Telephone .(604) 822-5858

Continuing Education (one-day gardening seminars)
Telephone (604) 822-2181

University of Washington
Elisabeth C. Miller Horticulture Library
Center of Urban Horticulture (Attn: Librarian)
GF-15, Seattle, WA., USA 98195
Telephone (206) 543-8616

Royal Botanical Gardens
Box 399, Hamilton, Ontario L8N 3H8

Royal Botanical Gardens Centre
680 Plains Road, West, Burlington, Ontario

Chicago Botanical Gardens
Box 400, Glencoe, IL, 60022-0400

SUPPLIERS OF GREENHOUSES AND ACCESSORIES

Greenhouses and equipment are available through the following selected firms. These companies have catalogues listing all their products.

B.C. Greenhouse Builders Co. Ltd.
7425 Hedley Ave., Burnaby, B.C., V5E 2R1
Telephone (604) 433-4220

Jacobs Greenhouses
371 Talbot Road, Delhi, Ontario, N4B 2A1
Telephone (519) 582-2880

Charley's Greenhouse Supplies
1569 Memorial Highway,
Mt. Vernon, WA. U.S.A. 98273
Telephone 1-800-322-4707

Gardener's Supply Company
128 Intervale Road,
Vermont, U.S.A. 05401
Telephone 1-800-688-5510

SELECTED BIBLIOGRAPHY

Crockett, James Underwood. Greenhouse Gardening As A Hobby. New York: Doubleday & Company, 1961.

Goold-Adams, Deenagh. The Cool Greenhouse Today. London: Faber & Faber Ltd., 1964.

Goold-Adams, Deenagh. The Small Greenhouse. Revised by Ray Waite. London: The Royal Horticultural Society, 1989.

Hessayon, D.G. Be Your Own Greenhouse Expert. Herts, England: PBI Publications, 1990.

Jones, Carolyn. The Complete Guide To Bedding Plants For Amateurs and Experts. Vancouver: Whitecap Books, 1989.

Lammers, Susan M. All About Houseplants. San Francisco: Ortho Books, 1982.

Simple Greenhouse Gardening. Edited by Alan Toogood. London: Ward Lock Ltd., 1987.

Tarrant, David. A Year In Your Garden. Vancouver: Whitecap Books, 1989.

About the Author

Greta Heinen was raised in a family of gardeners and has always had a keen interest in gardening. She is a homemaker and co-owner of a greenhouse manufacturing firm. As a result, her love for gardening became more specialized in the field of greenhouse gardening. Greta has used her experience and knowledge in teaching courses for Continuing Education in Burnaby. She also continues to contribute articles to *Gardens West* magazine.

ORDER FORM

To: Birch Publishing
P.O. Box 32092
Langley, B.C.
CANADA
V1M 1L9

Ship to:_____

Name:_____

Address:_____

City:_____

Postal Code:_____

Telephone:_____

Telephone Orders:　　**(604) 882-0068**
Fax Orders-Fill out this form and
fax to:　　　　　　　**(604) 882-8760**

Please have your Visa or Mastercard
ready for phone or fax orders.

Card #:_____

Exp.date____/____

Signature_____

Postal Orders:
I am enclosing $_____
Please charge my ( ) Visa or ( ) MC

In Your Greenhouse Book	$ 8.95
Mailing Charges　$1.75 (Canada)	$____
$2.25 (U.S.A.)	$____
Subtotal	$____
Add 7% GST (Canadian Residents)	$____
Total	$____

75